How to understand the Jewish religious
sacrifices described in Leviticus

Rising Smoke

An inductive Bible teaching series
for individuals or groups

by Douglas Parrington

1 – The Burnt Offering

Rising Smoke, Book 1 – The Burnt Offering
Published by NENGE BOOKS, Australia
ABN 26809396184
Email: nengebooks1@gmail.com

Unless otherwise indicated, Scripture quotations are taken from the Holy Bible, New Living Translation, copyright© 1996. Used by permission of Tyndale House Publishers, Inc. Wheaton, Illinois 60189. All rights reserved.

Copyright © Douglas Parrington 2015
All rights reserved.

Available from Christian bookstores or order direct from the publisher at website: http://nengebooks.com or email: nengebooks1@gmail.com

Douglas Parrington MA is a former teacher who was also a Bible Translator in the Notu-Ewage language of Oro Province, Papua New Guinea. This study is the first of a series that considers the Old Testament sacrifices in Leviticus in the light of their fulfilment in the New Testament. It is designed as a self-study guide for individuals and groups who wish to improve their understanding of the Old Testament and its fulfilment in Christ.

ISBN 978-0-9925620-2-1

Rising Smoke – Study 1: The Burnt Offering

Contents

ACCEPTANCE WITH GOD   5

1. THE OFFERING WAS PROVIDED BY THE PEOPLE   7

2. THE OFFERING WAS TO BE WITHOUT ANY DEFECT   8

3. GOD ACCEPTED THE OFFERING AS A SUBSTITUTE   10

4. THE OFFERING MAKES ATONEMENT FOR SIN   12

5. THE OFFERING IS PLEASING TO THE LORD   14

6. DIFFERENT WAYS OF THINKING ABOUT IT   16

7. A PERSONAL REFLECTION   20

Endnotes   22

Rising Smoke – Study 1: The Burnt Offering

ACCEPTANCE WITH GOD

Deep down inside us we have all felt a longing to be accepted. We want people around us who accept us, who help us grow in our physical, emotional and spiritual lives.

Dr Garry Collins[1] has this to say about the reason many people do not experience that acceptance:

> Parents communicate acceptance in a variety of ways; by touching, by spending time with their children, by listening, by discipline, by showing affection. When these clues are missing, or when children are ignored or excessively criticized, they begin to feel worthless. They begin to conclude that they don't belong and they either withdraw from others or force themselves on others in a way that brings more rejection. It then becomes difficult to trust people and this inability to trust prevents close relationships from forming.
>
> We who are older respond in similar ways when we do not feel accepted. Parents who feel they are no longer accepted or wanted by their children, spouses who feel rejected by their mates, pastors who feel unappreciated by their congregations, or employees who feel shunned by their employers and co-workers—all are examples of people who feel unaccepted, not needed, and often lonely.

In your culture, what makes people feel that they are accepted or rejected?

✍

Are there times in which you personally do not feel accepted by the people around you? Why?

✍

Rising Smoke – Study 1: The Burnt Offering

An even deeper need we have is to feel that God accepts us. The people of Israel were able to find that acceptance through the sacrificial offerings.

📖 **Read Leviticus 1:1-17.**

What do you learn about finding acceptance with God from this chapter?

✎

Can we expect to find anything of significance today in the sacrifices described for us in Leviticus? Allen Ross[2] tells us that we can.

> The Biblical descriptions of sacrifices represent a complex system of ritual worship that is not entirely clear to the modern reader. This is partly due to the texts legislating and describing activities that span centuries, naturally involving change and developing within the prescribed ritual. It is also due to the biblical accounts not explaining the meaning of much of the material, apparently assuming that people would either know by experience or learn through Levitical instruction the reasons for all the details (Deuteronomy 33:10, Malachi 2:7).
>
> For us, what has been made clear in Scripture provides a framework for the interpretation of the details ... All the sacrifices that were given to Israel find their fulfilment in the death of the Son of God on the cross—that was the plan all along ... And in the fullness of time their true significance became clear in God's plan of redemption.

As we come now to explore the features of the burnt offering, let's look for elements in it that point us to the sacrificial death of Christ.

📖 Read carefully John's description of Jesus in John 1:29b.

How does John describe Jesus? Compare this with Leviticus 1:10. Is there anything the same?

✎

Here are some features of the Burnt Offering to look for:

1. THE OFFERING WAS PROVIDED BY THE PEOPLE

📖 Read Leviticus 1:2.

The offering was to come from among the people—from the cattle, sheep, or birds they owned. What about Jesus, did he come from among the people?

📖 Read John 1:14 and Philippians 2:5-11.

What do these verses tell us about Jesus and how he lived?

✎

2. THE OFFERING WAS TO BE WITHOUT ANY DEFECT

The people needed to choose the offering carefully. It was to be without a defect or blemish of any sort. We take this to mean in personality as well as physically. The Lord gives this further instruction to Moses to pass on to the people.

📖 **Read Leviticus 1:3 & 10. How does Jesus meet the requirements for the Leviticus offerings according to the following passages:**

2 Corinthians 5:21

✎

1 Peter 1:18-20

✎

Hebrews 4:15

✎

Hebrews 9:13-14

✎

Notice how Peter in his letter tells us that God had planned 'long before the world began' that Christ would become the sacrificial offering for sin. John writes of him as 'the lamb who was killed before the world was made.' (Revelation 13:8b). This is why we can say that God saw the sacrificial death of Christ in the sacrificial offerings presented by the people of Israel. The sacrificial death of Christ was foreshadowed in those former offerings. One New Testament writer puts it this way ...

> The old system in the law of Moses was only a shadow of the things to come, not the reality of the good things Christ has done for us. The sacrifices under the old system were repeated again and again, year after year, but they were never able to provide perfect cleansing for those who came to worship. (Hebrews 10:1)

📖 Read Hebrews 10:11-12

The writer explains that Jesus did more than what the Old Testament priests did. They only presented an offering to God. He did more than that. Notice also how the writer refers to Christ as 'our High Priest.' As you think about the following question, can you see why?

As our High Priest, what has Jesus done for us?
✍

Forgiveness was still possible under the former system however because God saw the sacrificial death of Christ on the cross pictured in those sacrifices.

3. GOD ACCEPTED THE OFFERING AS A SUBSTITUTE

📖 Read Leviticus 1:4.

The Concise Oxford Dictionary defines a substitute as 'a person performing some function instead of another,' or 'something put in exchange for something else.' In the burnt offering, the priest presented the sacrifice on behalf of the person. The animal took the death penalty instead of the person who had sinned.

What did people have to do in order for God to accept the sacrifice as a substitute for them?

✍

📖 Read John 1:12.

How does the Old Testament picture of Leviticus 1:4 help us understand what John says in this verse about Christ? How do we 'lay a hand' on him? Or to ask the question in another way, using John's language, 'What do we need to do to become a child of God?"

✍

Here's a question to think about while moving on in the study: Why is a substitute needed?

Rising Smoke – Study 1: The Burnt Offering

📖 **Read Genesis 2:15-17, Ezekiel 18:4 & Romans 6:33**

What does God say is the penalty for disobeying him?

✎

It is we sinful people who are under the sentence of death because of our sins. When Jesus Christ received the death penalty he took our place. He was there on the cross instead of us.

📖 **Read Isaiah 53:4-6, Romans 5:8-9 and 1 Corinthians 5:7.**

According to these verses, who did Jesus suffer and die for?

✎

📖 **Read again Leviticus 1:4**

Notice what the burnt offering accomplished for the people and how they responded. Laying hands on the burnt offering was the way people showed that they believed the sacrifice was being made on their behalf. It was an indication of faith. Faith brought the assurance that their sins were now atoned for. This is what the burnt offering is all about.

4. THE OFFERING MAKES ATONEMENT FOR SIN

How are we to understand the term 'atonement'? The Hebrew word is *kaphar*. Its basic meaning is 'to cover'. It is derived from the word *kopher*, 'the price of a life, a ransom.' Based on the meaning of these two Hebrew words, Charles Swindoll[3] defines atonement this way.

> ATONEMENT: An all-inclusive word that describes, in general, all that Jesus Christ accomplished by his death on the cross. The term is found only in the Old Testament, where it means 'to cover' and carries with it the thought of putting sin out of sight, covering it over by blood.

In the word atonement we find the idea of God's anger being satisfied by means of a sacrificial offering. The phrase, *'to satisfy God's anger against us'*, found here in the New Living Translation which follows, gives us the actual meaning of the word.

> For all have sinned and come short of God's glorious standard. Yet now God in his gracious kindness declares us not guilty. He has done this through Christ Jesus, who has freed [redeemed] us by taking away our sins. For God sent Jesus to take the punishment for our sins and to satisfy God's anger against us. (Romans 3:23-26).

We must remember that God is perfect in the expression of all his emotions whereas we are imperfect. In expressing his wrath or anger God remains holy. We are anything but perfect in the expression of ours. John Stott[4] helps us understand the nature of God's anger when he reminds us that 'sin arouses the wrath of God.'

> This does not mean, (as animists fear) that he is likely to fly off the handle at the most trivial provocation, still less that he loses his temper for no apparent reason at all. For there is nothing capricious or arbitrary about the holy God. Nor is he ever irascible, malicious, spiteful or vindictive. His anger is neither mysterious or irrational. It is never unpredictable, but always predictable, because it is provoked by evil and evil alone. The wrath of God ... is his steady, unrelenting, unremitting, uncompromising antagonism to evil in all its forms and manifestations. In short, God's anger is poles apart

Rising Smoke – Study 1: The Burnt Offering

from ours. What provokes our anger (injured vanity) never provokes his; what provokes his anger (evil) seldom provokes ours.

The atonement made possible by the burnt offering has been fully realised in the sacrificial death of Christ.

📖 **Read 1 John 2:1-2.**

What does John say about Jesus' work of atonement?

✎

It is important to remember that it is God who takes the initiative in all of this. The atoning sacrifice, in both the burnt offering and Christ's sacrificial death, is a gift from God. It is God who is making the atoning sacrifice, not us. We do not present it, God does on our behalf. John Stott[5] explains it for us …

> In a pagan context it is always human beings who seek to avert the divine anger either by the meticulous performance of rituals, or by the recitation of magical formulae, or by the offering of sacrifices (vegetable, animal, or even human). Such practices are thought to placate the offended deity. But the gospel begins with the outspoken assertion that nothing we can do, say, offer or even contribute can compensate for our sins or turn away God's anger. There is no possibility of persuading, cajoling or bribing God to forgive us, for we deserve nothing at his hands but judgement. Nor, as we have seen, has Christ by his sacrifice prevailed on God to pardon us. No, the initiative has been taken by God himself in his sheer mercy and grace.

Rising Smoke – Study 1: The Burnt Offering

This was already clear in the Old Testament, in which the sacrifices were recognized not as human works but as divine gifts. They did not make God gracious; they were provided by a gracious God in order that he might act graciously towards his sinful people. 'I have given it to you', God said of the sacrificial blood, 'to make atonement for yourselves on the altar' (Leviticus 17:11). And this truth is yet more plainly recognized in the New Testament, not least in the three main texts about propitiation (atonement).[6] God himself 'presented' (NIV) or 'put forward' (RSV) Jesus Christ as a propitiatory (atoning) sacrifice (Romans 3:25). It is not that we loved God, but that he loved us and sent his Son as a propitiation (atonement) for our sins (1 John 4:10). It cannot be emphasised too strongly that God's love is the source, not the consequence of the atonement.

As P. T Forsyth[7] expressed it, 'the atonement did not procure grace, it flowed from grace.' God does not love us because Christ died for us; Christ died for us because God loved us. If it is God's wrath that needed to be propitiated, it is God's love which did the propitiating.

In the comment above, John Stott is taking the word 'propitiation' from an old English translation of the Scriptures. The word carries the same meaning as the word 'atonement.'

5. THE OFFERING IS PLEASING TO THE LORD

God gave detailed instructions for the priests about how they were to present the burnt offering.

📖 **Read Leviticus 1:9-17.**

What are the priests instructed to do with the sacrifice?
✍

How does God feel about this sacrifice?

✍

📖 **Read Psalm 40:6-10 and Hebrews 10:1-10**

What was it about the sacrifice that pleased God?

Was it the offering itself that God was pleased with, or something else? What can you find in the above Scriptures to answer this question?

✍

📖 **Read Hebrews 11:6.**

What do we need to do to please God?

✍

Rising Smoke – Study 1: The Burnt Offering

📖 **Read Psalm 51:10, 16-17.**

David realised the sinfulness of his recent life style and asked the Lord for forgiveness.

What does David tell us that God looks for in a person's attitude? How does he describe the kind of sacrifice that God is pleased with?

✎

You may be wondering just now what the people's response to the Lord's instructions concerning the burnt offering may have been. In such a large community we would expect that people would have ...

6. DIFFERENT WAYS OF THINKING ABOUT IT

6.1 A Superior Attitude

The offerings that poor people brought were just as acceptable to the Lord as those the wealthy brought. But some of the wealthier people who took their sacrificial offerings from the large herds they owned may have been tempted to look down on those who brought an offering from their small flock of sheep, or those who had only a bird to bring. They may have thought that they were superior because of the size of their herd or flock. An attitude like that could so easily lead to acts of discrimination in the community, like those which arose among some of the early Christians.

📖 **Read James 2:1-4.**

What does James say about discrimination? Is discrimination right? How do we discriminate against some people?

✍

People sometimes feel superior because of the status of the Christian leaders they follow or the denomination they belong to. Paul warned the members of the church in Corinth that this was just what was happening among them.

📖 **Read 1 Corinthians 3:3-5, 4:6-7**

What does Paul say is the reason for these superior feelings? What does he say is the way to overcome those feelings?

✍

Others may feel superior because of the spiritual gifts they had received, forgetting that different gifts[8] are given to people according to the ministry they are called to fulfil. No particular gift makes one person superior to the other. Paul writes of this in another of his letters.

📖 **Read Romans 12:3-11.**

What advice does Paul give to those who feel superior because of the spiritual gifts they have received?

6.2 Not Every Offering Is Acceptable to God

The animals offered were to be in perfect condition. But some people may have thought that it didn't matter what kind of offering they presented. For example, someone going out into the fields to choose an animal from the herd or flock might spot a sickly looking one and think, "that one is half dead anyway, it will do for the offering."

📖 Read Psalm 50:7-15.

What does God say in these verses about the sacrifices? Who owns the animals anyway? What does God really want?

✍

📖 Read Malachi 1:6-10.

What does God, through Malachi, say about the kind of sacrifices people were offering? How did God feel about this?

✍

6.3 Religious Syncretism

The term religious syncretism refers to the mixing of two or more religious beliefs and systems to try and gain maximum spiritual influence.

When they saw the way the Canaanites offered sacrifices to their gods, some of the Israelites may have thought it would be a good idea to mix what they considered to be the good elements of the Canaanite rituals with theirs.

It seems that religious syncretism created trouble for the church in Colosse. Both the Judaism of the Israelites and the Gnosticism of Greek philosophers had become entwined with Christian truth in the teaching of the false teachers who were troubling the members of the church. Herbert Carson[9] writes:

> The resultant religious amalgam (mixture) is an attempt to advance beyond apostolic Christianity. There is no suggestion that Christ is openly rejected. He still has a place; but only as one among many angelic powers.

Paul wrote to the church in Colosse to help them discern some of these errors.

📖 **Read Colossians 1:9-10, 2:6-10**

Paul gives several ways in which the Colossian Christians could remain strong in their faith. Find at least four of these in the above Scriptures.

✎

1.

2.

3.

4.

It may be helpful now to conclude our study together with …

7. A PERSONAL REFLECTION

'Type' is a term given to refer to something that presents a picture of or represents something else. Allen Ross[10] tells us that "Typology is a divinely prefigured illustration of a corresponding reality." With this definition in mind think back over what you have discovered in this first chapter of Leviticus.

What new things have you learnt about the death of Christ? In the Burnt Offering, is there a 'type' of Christ, features that present us with a picture of him?

✍

Rising Smoke – Study 1: The Burnt Offering

What new perspectives on the meaning of faith for a Christian have you learnt?

✍

How can you apply what you have learnt about what pleases God to your life and attitudes?

✍

Do you now feel accepted by the Lord? Do you feel comfortable in God's presence now? What makes you feel this way?

✍

Endnotes

[1] Collins, Gary R. CHRISTIAN COUNSELLING. England: Word (UK) Ltd. 1988. pp. 95-96.
[2] Ross, Allen P. HOLINESS TO THE LORD. A Guide To the Exposition of the Book of Leviticus. Michigan: Baker Academic. 2002. pp. 29-30, 33.
[3] Swindoll, Charles R. GROWING DEEP IN THE CHRISTIAN LIFE. Oregon: Multnomah Press. 1986. p. 413.
[4] Stott, John. THE ESSENTIAL JOHN STOTT. Combined Edition. The Cross Of Christ. The Contemporary Christian. England: IVF. 1999. p. 160.
[5] Stott. Ibid: p. 160
[6] For Stott's use of the term 'propitiation', found in older translations, read 'atoning sacrifice'.
[7] P. T. Forsyth, *Cruciality of the Cross,* p. 78. Compare Calvin's statement: 'The work of atonement derives from God's love, therefore it did not establish it' (*Institutes,* II.xvi.4).
[8] Refer to Romans 12:6-8; 1 Corinthians 12:1-11, 27-31; Ephesians 4:4-13.
[9] Carson, Herbert M. THE EPISTLES OF PAUL TO THE COLOSSIANS AND PHILEMON. Michigan: Tyndale Press. 1977. p. 17.
[10] Ross. Ibid: p. 96, footnote 23.

Email the author at nengebooks1@gmail.com with your feedback on this study, or order the next study in this series:

Book 2 - 'The Grain Offering – Dedication to God.' (Leviticus 2:1-16).

MY NOTES

www.ingramcontent.com/pod-product-compliance
Lightning Source LLC
Chambersburg PA
CBHW052137010526
44113CB00036B/2306